Unwrapped Presents

Darcy Rollow

ACKNOWLEDGMENTS

I would like to thank my parents for allowing me to chase after my dreams as a writer, my best friend for being here for me always, and my brother for being a support system like no other. I would also like to thank my favorite professor, Kendra Kopelke, for all she does for everyone she meets, and my poetry club. A special thank you to all the healers out there working to help get the world back on their feet after they have been kicked down, we need you, and I am grateful for you all in my life.

DEDICATION

This book is for anyone who has ever felt alone, broken, violated, or abused in some kind of way. I dedicate this book to you, and may it bring some kind of comfort in your healing process.

Table of Contents

Part I

(Ode to a Bruise) #1

You stay
within the
passing days,
gorging on lilacs,
puffing purples
& monogamous maroons.
Please find a host
on someone else's body.
I don't want memory
of his hands on me.

The sight of
you disgusts me.
Bile rising up
as if gravity has neglected me
as well.
Your outer shell,
green and yellow
my old school colors, but there
is nothing   spirited
about me wearing you.

Freckles inside, little miniature
bruises within one,
        as if
there was a world built
inside his palms, waiting
to kidnap me, waiting
to enslave my skin
for his pleasure
            only.

My friends tell me that
the mark has faded.
My brain says

the pain has receded.

But my eyes still see
the hand prints he left,
as if
     they
were almost
more significant   than my own.

#2

You are not here,
nor anywhere near my physical body.
But memories have a way
of conjuring what is not actually
physical.

No matter the distance,
the time I push between
us, you are here,
next to me.
The darkness keeps on clawing
me still, silent.

I wish I could rip
the sides of my scalp down,
unzipping this body
that I claim is "okay". Fold
the skin you touched,
and toss it away.

I wish I could scoop
memories of you out of this brain
like ice-cream.

You are here as
shadows in the corner
of my eyes, peeking around
door jambs, and thin walls—
I swear I can hear you singing
in my head, but you are
                down the hall.

I can hear your distant typing,
somewhere   within the figment of my imagination,
or what you look like dancing

to the rhythm of some forgotten
song you played each time
you were "gone".

And now you are really   gone,
haven't been around you
        since the night your body
opened mine.

You were an unwrapped gift
I didn't know
        I signed for, and I have regretted
receiving it
ever since.

#3

You were left aside,
I knew more about
your dark corners
than anyone had
ever tried.

I knew how the shadows
touched you in places
you thought darkness
could not harm, you thought
your mind at least, you had
            control of.

You were delivered
so nicely, all you had to do
was go beyond   those
who tried to wrap you
in different patterns, tried to wrinkle
and untie your essence, all you had
to do was shut them out.

But you were so broken,
when they sent your father
to jail, who could blame you?
The hits from Mama,
they did not help you either,
you kept breaking, reforming,
shattering, transforming—
until, you looked as if
you were a gift.

You *are* a gift.
We are all presents. But we are only
what we choose to be, we are
as beautiful as

what we choose to use our beauty for.
And this,
determines whether we
have been broken
or not.

#4

I live
three doors down from you.
You, who drugged my drink, nestled
your negativity in my chest, and tried to choke me of
all my dreams.

I live three doors down from the   monster
that proved to me that fears were real.
From you who   refuses
to take your pills
because they make you feel "foggy".

I live three doors down
from the people I wasted two months
of my life with. Three doors down,
in a trunk underneath the bed, are who knows
what kind of drugs you have given me before.

Three doors down, you laced me
so many times before, all those misinformed dreams—
hallucinations, …who knows how many times
you took my memory without me knowing?

Three doors down, and I haven't been back
since the night
you violated every inch
of my spirit and body.

Three doors down, and I still take a moment to peer around
the elevator doors in hopes
to not find you standing right there.
I have to speed down the hall, checking my back
every few steps
to make sure you aren't following me to my home

asking why
I never came back—
why I gave up on you, when I said
I would be the one person
that *wouldn't.*

Three doors down,
and I will never forget what happened there.
I will never be able to walk by without shivers
coating my spine, without flashbacks haunting my mind,
sharpening my eyes—
I won't forget you ever.

But isn't that what you wanted?
For your image   to last   forever?

#5

I used to be the girl
that always got away
        safe.
Should have been counting   my lucky stars,
        on a plane
        where I could confide in them,
rather than complain to them.

But instead;
I wiggled and whined
        asking the universe
        when it was My time
to experience,
to mess up, to learn,
        begging for moments
I could grow on my own
without a hand in someone
else's life.

Now I count my
mistakes, adding them up
        higher than my blessings,
wiggling and whining.
Why couldn't I stay a child,
        ignorant of all the growth
        I've had to go through?

Now I fight with my lungs,
        trying to remember how
I used to breathe.
        I remembered it used to be easy
to inhale, and let
go. Now, I have a hard time
        remembering that girl,
or what *safe* even feels like.

#6

You can't keep entering
my head,
and *fucking* everything.

#7

Arching back
so curvy—so pretty,
my spine,
          you used it almost
          like a whip
to bring that "scream"
you so liked.

My mouth knew words once,
          but lost the meaning—
          chokingchokingchoking
you're hurting me.

It wasn't meant to go
          like this.
You weren't meant
to think
          about your depression:
like dark paints
crusading your brain,   attacking
you heart in heart beat
rhythms and
explosive malnutrition.
          I only had two drinks. Why do I feel like this?
Wasn't supposed to be
          like that.
I was just trying to help
because I care
          from the bottom
          of my ocean
          back up to the top
          of my stars
for the broken hearts,
          the injured souls,
the restless thinkers,

because I was wishing
          silently, praying,
screaming
that someone would extend
the words   back to me.

#8

Punishing
      this body
      for rejecting you?

Legs
      stuck in   places
legs shouldn't go.

Bruises are
      watercolors
of lilac
      peonies, and hydrangeas…

Scar
      from your finger nails?
      Check the knife on his bedside table.

Did you stab me
      in the back
when I had no memory
of you doing so?

If I don't remember,
      do you think that means it doesn't count?

#9

I wanted
        the band aids
        you were offering
so badly, that
        I unzipped
        my palms
        so they would bleed
artwork,
        of abstract splashes.
        That way
you could offer
        a way to close
them back up.

But you wanted
        more from me than
        my wisdom of words
about your drug problem.
You wanted more
        than my warnings
        that you were harming yourself,
        You knew what you were doing and liked it.

        So instead,
        you zipped up my mouth,
and the only words I ever
heard were your
"Uh uh"'s in my head
        making me understand that
band aids would
        never
have been enough
anyway.

#10

Your destruction
follows behind me
        like a trail of bread crumbs
I know too well the directions
        of.

#11

 You were a
        screaming dream
I had forgotten years ago.
Crying
        in the middle of the night
        I was a child,
so afraid of the dark,
        without having reason to be
        back then.

But I woke
        to turning twenty-one,
crying
        in the morning
        as an adult,
to find you
creeping into my skin,
forever
        making me fear
the daylight
        more.

#12

Were you rolling
up your sins
and blowing out the dreams you didn't
pursue?
Did you
ignore your thoughts
and burn away
the bones of what was
left of the little boy
who once dared to dream?
Your parents made you hate the world
didn't they? So you
started doing the things
Daddy did
but he ended up in jail, steel
bars crossing over his heart
and jump suit
orange decorating
his pale soul.
Didn't he know
the burns would last
eons on your back?

Or was he too busy
shoving bottles
down his throat
obscuring the bottled
up feelings he was
told he wouldn't be missing?
Or were those
stored away in
ashtrays of ashy hearts
& unrequited love and
misguided lust
& mistrust &

doesn't he care?
&
Does he even know you?
& When
was the last time you saw his face?
&
To love
is to endure pain.
&
That's your hand
around my neck

&
You can't hear.
You can't feel.
You can't hear.
You're hurting me.
Can't hear.
Stop.
Can't feel
please.
&
Daddy's still in jail.
&
You wish
you were in
the ground.
&
Why doesn't anyone care?

Rolling up your life
is easy when it
fits so neatly
in a tobacco leaf, but
getting it to stay
in place is the real
task, and sometimes no matter

how many times
you lace it with
something else, you still
have the same
horrible high—
the one that tells you
when you're sober
you're still going to have to deal
with the shit when you're
back down,
so maybe
you won't come back down
ever.
&
Daddy's still in jail
&
you're not
&
I'm hurt
&
so are you
&
you aren't ever coming
down.
&
I'm too far
gone
to realize.

#13

For a moment,
I am stable. I am in this
collected bliss
where there are no whispers
        of wanting to disappear,
        of needing to forget.
I am in this
elusive moment
so   transparent
of the thought
I thought
I knew,
of the reality   in which
        I pursued.
        I am no longer aside
from the fears
that I thought
        were untrue.

For a moment,
I depended on you,
I begged
        myself to gain
        some experiences,
even if negative,
because I had to prove
to this beating   heart
        that I was *living*...

For a moment,
I was still.
I knew the language of stars.
I was aligned and so pure.
I was so true, and too happily unaware
        of the darkness

that surrounds us
in this world.

For a moment,
    I thought that no evil   would ever touch me.
But I fell
for the Devil himself.
Little did I know, his hands were already
claiming me
before
I even knew
that I was gasping
                        for air.
For a moment,
    I was dizzy,
I tried pulling air into my lungs
        but found that your hands were there
telling me,   "shh".
For a moment,
I remembered when we joked
about the fact
that abusing women turned you   on because your mom
violently hit you
        when you were a child.
For a moment, my eyes were blackened
behind the sheet
of veiled eyelids
        because for that moment
        that your hand choked me,
            I couldn't see,
            couldn't speak.

But I am speaking now.

Part II

(Don't/Leave Me Alone) #14

You stay,
please go.
I am
beside you.

                                  The passing days,

are heaven—
an unknown hell.

puffing   smoke
purple   pleasantries.
monogamous maroons
I wish
                      you didn't decide
                      my fate
                      for me.
Please
find
        someone else.
I don't
want memory
of your kindness
            staining me.

                              Rising up,
                              I did
                              once

until
your words
touched my ear,
"I'm going to end my life tonight."

No,
no.
How could
I not have stayed?

Why didn't the moon
climb out from under night's blanket,
and remove your hands
from around my neck?
          Why couldn't the stars
          shine their light
          warm enough to heal
          your wounds?

Was God listening
when you   took
                my voice from me?

There was a world
                        built
inside of you.

Why couldn't Baltimore
see into your little corner window,
          and pull me
          from the pond
          of your nails?

My skin itches
sometimes,
          right
          there, in that
          crescent slope
          of my right shoulder.

What were you waiting
for?
                Did you know what you were going to do?
                How come
                the red flags
                weren't as vibrant

        as the prints
        of your hands?

My brain says
the pain has   receded.

But my eyes
still see
      all he left,
as if
     they
have formed a new life
inside my skin;
you are always
with me—
please
go,
stay, leave,
don't.

Goodbye, *please.*

#15

I woke up the morning
       after my twenty first birthday
with the unwrapped present
of you and I
       in your bed
and a gash
on my shoulder
that I don't remember receiving.

I asked everyone
       what they saw.
       No one saw.
       No one
       but the sky
       witnessed my fall
                              that night.
No one knew
why I had *that*
on my shoulder.

No one knew
except for you who pointed it out
in the first place. Manipulation
       made you try to
       cover it up
       by hiding it in plain sight.
A fake smile,
phony surprise party of eyes.
Your thoughts:
we hadn't done anything
wrong.

Your thoughts:
this is college
       and women have sex

with men when they're too
drunk.

Isn't that what you tried to tell me?
Told me that I ran to your room
after a few shots and
begged you to come inside me?
That I kept
            shouting your name
from your bedroom
when a room full of people
were there to celebrate
                my birthday.

Isn't that what you told me?
"You wanted it."
"This was your plan all along."
Did I nod my head
because I was confused and scared?
            Or did I scream 'no'? My memory
wouldn't know.
Didn't you tell me that you had no idea
where the scar had come from?
Didn't you put Neosporin on it
so it wouldn't become infected?

Didn't you tell me
you liked me, more than a best friend?
Didn't you tell me
that you could get me any way you wanted?

And why didn't I know at all
what you were really saying?

#16

It's funny.
I still see you
as a human being
sometimes.

Innocently, dancing
to a tune, with a mop in hand.
But you never asked me
to dance with you,
and I thought it was
beautiful that
you didn't.

It's funny.
I have to tell my face
to *not* smile, to not remember you
like that,
to remember what you did.

You acted like a young boy,
as you cuddled your dog,
          rubbing his fur
with love in your
hands. You just wanted
a normal life.
You didn't ask
for your upbringing,
didn't want to have to sell
drugs to pay for your tuition.
You didn't want to get lost in it,
little boy.
You didn't tell your father
to do what he did.
Little boy, I know your heart
believes you are just as bad

as him
because you have
the same blood,
    the same *needs*.

Little boy, I see your   heart even though
it is covered up
    pretty well.
I see the scars in which
your mother's hand left
on your skin.
I feel the twitches
vibrating through your   body,
from the times you banged you head
    against the wall
    hoping to rattle a voice alive
telling you that *you can, this your own life.*
Hoping that the skull hitting
plaster would manipulate you into
ecstasy,
    and when it didn't
you hoped it
    would put an end to the voice
forever telling you that
    you can't.

Little boy, you were so young
when they told you
that you could be nothing.
It became a religion you
you chose to follow.
    But in my company, you sought out
other religions,
you wanted to be different.

And when I let you know
that you could not be mine,

you took my neck into your own
hands, and shoved all your heartbreak into
my lungs, hoping I would stop breathing
        for long enough
to understand
        how many times
you wanted not to.
But you cannot strangle yourself,
only others can do that.
I learned that   from you.

#17

How many more times must
I whisper,
"You're okay," before
I stop replying back,
"I'm not."

#18

"How've U Been?" He texts me.
I want to reply—
oh you mean since you drugged me?
How have I been since the night
I was high   off my brain cells
with you and your five friends,
and their hungry eyes, waiting
to explore what might occur
next?
How have I been
since I started
wounding myself as self-punishment
due to having your dark energy
              forced inside of me?

"How've U Been?"
Since March 5th?
Since your buddies
peered at my body
stripping away the clothing
imagining things for themselves
like what you told them,
like how you ripped
my soul away from me
during so many parties.

How have I been?
You mean since you smashed
every single fragile
and true thing I knew about myself?
How have I been since
every cell was tormented
with a new strategy
each day trying
to win over my mind—

so I couldn't feel anymore?
How have I been since
the thought of you taking pills
        made me think it was good idea?
How have I been
        since every day waking
up I had to   fight the self that told me
        to stay down?

How am I?
How am I?
You mean since you corrupted
my belief in God?
Since you coated my energy
in anger?

How am I?
You mean since
not being able to walk down
my hallway without fear?
You mean since always having
to wear a hood in the city praying you wouldn't see me?
Even if it was hot outside?
Even if no one else recognized me?
You mean since
        the day I haven't been able to
recognize myself?

How am I?
Since I   almost took my own life?
Since I started binge drinking
my emotions, because to *feel*
        is too much?

How have I been?
Since I've been avoiding you and
all of your ten friends?

So you couldn't ask me fake questions
trying to determine if I knew or not—
trying to see if I was
still so
naive
like I was
when you told me
that you
liked
me.

That
we
fit
together.

But I didn't
want to fit inside
you.
But you made sure that
I did.

"I'm doing well. Thanks."

#19

Do you know what it feels like
            to confront the Devil,
and lose?

Do you know what it feels like to be roofied?
And to have some part of yourself know
that this isn't right.
            Do you know how it feels when
the alarm goes off in
your stomach, and you want to vomit
but can't because
the muscle relaxer has already started to work? And
what few thoughts you have left start to—

Do you know what it's like
            to try and cling on to the   words
to try
to form sentences
to save yourself, your body, and your mind?

It started with my feet,
I felt the soles of them hop
            from my heel to ankle.
I felt the circle of my calves
shake as they lay limb, waiting for what comes next.
            Then the red flags that often
slept in my stomach that I had ignored,
 became vibrant,
            strong.
If I can just move my hands.

            Yes! Fleeting thought, catch it   before
madness happens. If I can just…

What was it? Stomach is

rebelling, a voice in my head: *leave here now.*
        Where am I? Why is it so dark?
Why are people filtering out of
the room?

If I can just move my hands I can text someone for help.

Just move hands, move like
you never have before,
 run the race, you've been training for this.
Slowly, they move,
fast for a tortoise who wants
to win. Please
        let me win
        this time.
        It counts more than
        before.

Hands don't work like they should,
You leaned over, so I mouthed, "mom"
through my lips, and
you ignored the lit-up phone screen
for that reason. And I hate
        that I am grateful for your
childhood for this reason.

        I remember the exact text to my friend:
Come get me, just say you need
        a tampon, keep it casual,
and he was in so much fury,
        when she took my hand and
lugged me out of there.

Some days, I still live in that room
        in between
those white and grey sheets,
I didn't know how much someone

could have nightmares about a bed comforter.
I didn't realize how much
        I would remember the little things,
like incense, or dog food, or the Pink Floyd *Dark
Side of the Moon* banner on your left living room wall.

I don't want to remember those.
I want to feel,
I want to love, breathe, and thrive.
        But I can still feel the spirit of
that numbness creeping up my body
and when that happens,
the only thing I can do is—
        keep writing, keep hitting keys…

If I can just move my hands…

#20

Paranoia grips
my throat right where—   ignore it,
don't think about it,
He can't hurt me anymore.

Yes I can.

Cautiously checking my
        locks before
entering my room,
making sure the front door slammed shut
        so you can't get in
if you needed to.
I know you won't.
        Will you try?
        Will you try to own me again?

Have you started preying
on someone younger again?
Last girl was seventeen,
and you twenty. You posed
as her father to pick
        her up from high school
I should have known.
Should have known better.

Thoughts wrap around my
        neck like snug hands that
won't let go, and I
am coughing,
        it isn't real, this flashback.
Calm yourself down,
he is not here.

Yes I am.

His ghost makes footprints
        behind my back, scratching at the
layers of skin.
He can't get in.   *But I already have.*

#21

I was   up there,

at one point.
        I was happy, because we
were happy.

Two friends,
sun glasses shading the light
from our eyes, but keeping
        all the light
from ever getting in…too.

High enough to touch
the stars,
        but too far from heaven,
too cold for the sun,
yet too close
to the ice wars
being brawled between fallen angels.
They pelted us with their
        kindred souls,
crying
remembering
what it meant to be too high,
        falling
falling,
                falling
but never hitting ground.
Making commitments, I knew
wouldn't end well.

Remember when we got in the car,
smoked a long
pipe three nights in a row,
then drove the next morning

to go drink?

I was confronted by the Sun, then.
A talking source told me to   stop,
and my legs didn't want to leave
without me,
so I sat in that
damn too warm of a car,
and you were mad, because
we drove all that way.
Gas money is expensive for college students,
but so is weed.

I wasted it with my paranoid mind,
telling me things
I didn't want to hear like,
    what happened to you last night?
    And a lot of "I don't know"s in too many rows.

We couldn't get out of the car,
    and you hated me for it.
Friends that meant nothing,
meant so much. Significance that
was way too draining to mean anything real.
    How does meaning even mean anything,
if all it is just a group of mean words linked together like hands
    that never rehearsed
what they were going to do
before they grabbed you—

and shoved me into the wall.
Do you remember
how it felt to have that woman's body
under your complete control?
You said I asked for this.

I would *never* ask for this.

I would never let you
        slip me something consciously,
I thought we were friends.
        You wanted to be more.
I rejected you.
        Your ego was damaged.
But you wanted me regardless
        of my opinion.

I would never let you
        remove the knife from your bed stand,
and carve your anger out on me.
I would never have let
you near this body.

So far from heaven,
too close to the ground,
not centered enough,
I am being buried alive.

We were in the car that day,
and you hated me for being responsive
to the drug
        in a way that I wasn't before.

You hated me for so   much more
        than I ever even knew about.

But you loved me too.
        And what the hell   am I supposed to do with that now?

Part III

(Always Forever & Never Again) #22

You stay
for as long
as you like. A guest
uninvited.

You left
me

with
you.

Violence was not
permitted, but
you did so
          anyway.
Please
let me—speak.
You're hurting me.

          Blackouts
          unexplained. There
          is nothing

          here
          for you anymore,
          my wholeness you sabotaged,
          the moment
          your feet
          stepped through my heart.

Night doesn't
allow slumber
for a girl
          who cannot
remember.

Instead, birthday gifts
that I missed—are delivered
late,
in flashbacks,
screams under the moon,
and subconscious
memories being   torn
from shelves of brain that were presumed not functioning.

But you
made my body
a home,
        I wasn't
        aware of your arrival, nor
        the length of your stay.
        Yet,
        I started to feel
        like the guest
        in my own skin,
        who overstayed their welcome.

You learned to love
by pain—and I dare not
try to humanize   it.

My brain
says
the pain
            has receded.
            You like pain, don't you?

But my eyes
    still see
the hand prints
            he left.

        You shouldn't punch walls.

50

You shouldn't
have
done this to me...

As if *they*
were almost more significant   than my own.

#23

I want to crawl
          inside my own skin
and hide from you there.
          But even there, you have been.
          I think I remember you sucking
on the tomorrows of my bones.
Seething when
          my heart beat, beat against you like fists.
Heart fought back, that fire of warrior of mine,
                    thank god someone tried to.

I once witnessed,
          when your words reached
          inside my throat, and replaced mine with yours.
 You took my voice box
          and unplugged it from
the walls of my soul, because if no one could hear me
scream,
          then they don't know what you've accomplished,
          right?

I vaguely know the times
          when you butchered my brain
with misconceptions, you guessed were correct,
          like using my kindness against me,
remember that?
          I vaguely recall the time you perfected
the "right amount" of trust, the
          "right" amount of self-loathing,
the right stories to tell, and which
to withhold, which ones
          would get me to stay, which ones
          wouldn't chase me into the night.

I want to crawl into the hairs

on my arm, and give myself a hug,
for all the times I was left cold,
shivering, and uncertain.
When did skin develop seasons? And why
was my body a winter that could not be heated?

What did you leave me with?
Strands of skin hanging
off of these bones
like morbid flags torn and shredded—
saying yes, I survived
but just *barely*.

You left me
with the broken parts, expecting me to
expertly know how to fit them
back together. Presuming I would
know just what to do
the bleeding nails, the videos of words not formed,
the tattered shoulder blades,
a scar so small—one might mistake it
for a birth mark, yet so large
one might mistake it   for a comet.

But I wasn't born this way,
and I see it every damn day.
I see it when I am trying to face myself
in that mirror,
repeating daily, "It's not your fault".
I know it is there when people say
"You have a scar," and I say back,
"Yeah." Because I don't want to explain.

I laugh it off, because it's *funny*.
It's so very funny
the way that life can fuck you up
within a short amount of time.

The way a man can turn
your insides outward,
hanging them to dry   on a clothes line,
        but they never do. Funny, how they keep
twisting in knots
        so your guts show you just
how non-brave you really are,
        or maybe never were.

#24

Crime scene tape
        is wrapped around my heart,
warning anyone who comes near of
        what lurks beneath, steer clear. It's strange
now to think
what we did to our bodies.

        Silly, they didn't take
your fingerprints,
I should have recorded
them down somewhere.
        Your last name I still remember,
but try as I might
to search for you
        in days of raging need of revenge—
        I can't find.
It's as if
        you weren't real
        at all.

        Remember how the rug
came up and off the floor?
Like a torn-out tongue who
        wanted to be reacquainted with its owner.
Careful now,
        I may reawaken from my
disposition on the floor, the tape
around my body, white, telling stories of
        what killed me…

Sometimes I wonder
if I died, that night,
        and this is all just a goofed delusion
called "heaven", allowing me to "live" my life
the way I

would have wanted.
Perhaps reality is just a second chance,
and maybe
we are all already
dead.

#25

Night seems to peel
back the wards of my brain
        and I feel it
all   too much.
I guess I didn't
spell them as greatly as   I thought.

I thought cutting off my hair
        was getting rid of the dead
pieces of self that I had left
over from you.
        I thought becoming fit
changed my body so I could
run fast enough so
the   flashbacks wouldn't catch up
with me.
        I thought dying my hair light
would push away the darkness.

I thought changing my poems,
        changing my words,
standing up for self,
meant that I wouldn't experience
        the wounds of the girl
        who lay still;
who couldn't get off of the bed.
I thought punching walls
        instead of cutting palms
meant that I was doing better.

Night creeps   into my veins
blowing up the blood
        so it induces headaches, so these
knees can't hold me up. So that I cannot rise—

I thought that when the sun levitated
this morning,
        it would mean I wouldn't
feel the mistakes I made when
Night began to haunt my thoughts.

#26

There are days
when rocks
        pelt my back, like long lost
stars hoping to make amends.
Yet punishment is too far gone,
        in the lengths of time
        I've passed.

There are days when
        the sun breathes
        fire into my mouth, and with it
I can *speak*.
        But there are also times
        when breath
        purges out of my being
and with it—I remember
the times
I've struggled for
        air.

There are days
        when I look at things;
        and your name appears in autocorrect,
and it's like
an apparition of self-demise
        I wish could
be forgotten but is
disguised specifically, a gift from
        You—one unwrapped,
        waiting on my doorstep.

And you know how creepy
your skeleton bone hands
        used to hold mine, crushing
        my body into sand

for the hour glass to spill
out my guts for
myself to witness.

It doesn't matter how loud you talk,
if they don't want to listen.

And why aren't you listening?
Why doesn't anyone listen?
I have to climb up
through the windows of each and every one's
eyes, I have to sit beside
their souls,
even then it isn't enough.
Even then the fire doesn't blaze, it just burns,
and the destruction
of my bones
turns to ash.

Why didn't she see me when I was
on that cold tiled floor
of our kitchen? When my heart
was spread out like butter,
weak and thin, I handed it to you, don't you see?
She walked away.

Mother,
don't leave me like this,
grasping at breaths my lungs cannot filter.
Mother, remember who I was as a child,
I didn't mean
to grow into this person.
Don't you understand, who I am?

Can't you see my blazing soul
for what it is, not the body
that it's wrapped in? Not the eyes that weep

from terrors you refuse to hear about?
Can't you recognize my mind, not the one
that worries every time
I step out the door?

Don't you see the person, me, trying,
struggling, striving?

Mother, don't you see your baby?
the one you held so close in your arms,
right in front of Heart Center?
Don't you see her, somewhere within this
body you don't understand?

Don't you want to keep your promise,
the one you made with the world, when you said
you would protect her from all harm?
What about harm from myself?
Mother, do you hear me?
What about the bruises on my arms—
mother, can you save me from him?
What about the blackouts, mother do you
remember?
Did I call you that night?
What about the scars, momma, do you see them?
Do you think I'm healed yet?
Mommy…

I need you.
But you shut   me out.
I need to feel
the warmth of anything
radiating from you.

"Mom, are you listening?"
"Oh sorry, I was texting. What were you saying?"

Mother, do you remember
    when you told me I could tell you anything? Or
when I told you I would, and you said
kids only say 80% of the truth?

Mother,
    I'm trying to tell you it all,
    but you aren't listening.
And I need   someone to listen.

"Never mind it wasn't important."

#27

Your nails
        bit bruises
like sapphire petals
        staining ink
that blazes beneath my skin.

Your nails
crack fire
        hustling what
my innocent mind
learned was just another
trick
to get me to stay—
a little while longer.

Blossoming
        cherries upon lips
blood, I could taste, wish I could forget
what it meant to kiss—
and damn,
my heart for believing
you needed some
kind   of saving.

Perspiration
        flew out of
my mouth, I awoke in the middle
of the night with you
inside, you told me
to be quiet,
not too scream. Oh, was I being too loud?

Maybe it was
my drunken mind
orgasming like a betrayal

to self,
or perhaps
it was my soul screaming,
that   this choice
I did not allow.

You're still
in the slope of my neck,
curling your forsaken
claws against my pulse.

Thank God, I learned
how to shut up
that night,
it makes sense
why people have been
teaching me
to do so all of
my life.

#28

Daddy,
do you hear me scream at night?
Do you hear the girly voice?
Even as I fight for you to see the adult in my eyes,
I still need you.
Don't you see the tears engraved in my face
like a stone statue, permanent?

I keep trying, Daddy,
don't you think that's enough?
You don't know how bad it hurt me,
how the ache inside me whimpers:
each time someone lets me go,
each time someone ignores me,
each time they abuse me. It's like a whip to the heart,
and all these slashes
just keep building a home inside of me.

I keep trying, Dad,
in school I'm doing really well,
and you say
I'm smart
because transitioning to college is hard,
and on the outside
I have straight A's,
but on the inside—I'm failing.

I keep trying, Dad.
Where are your wrinkly hands to catch my dreams
falling out of my eyes?
I thought you were my dream catcher,
holding onto the ones that
I keep giving up on?
Your kind voice tells me,
it's okay, you're safe now. *But I don't believe you.*

Your stern one tells me it is their fault.
Your doctor one says that I was violated.

I keep trying, Father.
but these days, I don't know the man
who sits across from me
staring at his computer screen,
I don't understand the brilliant man
who discusses psychology with me.
I only remember the one
who used to play dolls with me as a child,
who kept trying each time
I picked up a new hobby to be part of it.

I guess you only
remember that little girl,
and let me tell you,
I wish I was her too.

#29

Take your claws
        and peel back the skin
        that cages my heart
from yours.

We weren't meant
        to connect like this,
        your organ being placed
within the confines
        of my ribs, you're the type
        that must be held captive,
        but you thought the same of me.

Because prison
        is the only place
that holds dangerous people, right?
        That's what you said when
you talked of your father.
        And you didn't want to be like him, so they
put him in a place
he couldn't touch,
couldn't hurt
again. And you
told me
you had tendencies
just as
he
did.

Were you trying…
        to kill me? It's not something
I like to think
about often.
I know you could have,
if I didn't stop talking that night.

Within the bars of
my own mind, I swear
that I bang the half full
        glass of my heart against these walls, making music
        with voices in the night, my voice—
tangled up with spirits
I don't recognize.
        Let me out   of here.
Why do you get to
walk so freely?
How do your feet plant
on earth, and you don't worry
        about which places they step?

How do you walk in daylight
        with the deeds done before dawn?
        How can you deceive all so well, is it because
you are so good at lying to yourself?

Take your fingers and dig
        for the treasure you thought might be inside.
If you couldn't visibly see it on the
outside already. Take your fingers
and *dig*.

Dig for whatever you like,
there is nothing left
after you.

But I have
                locked up this chest for quite
awhile now, and even though
I am so very lonely…
I've never felt safer.

#30

Mother,
I'm so tired.
My eyelids droop down to my nose
and all the way back up.
My tears collect inside of the grooves
like ancient waters
warming to the desert heat of my face.
Can this water ever be used again?

Mother,
I'm so angry,
these fists won't shut up
as they hit the walls, loudly
showing my neighbors there is something wrong next door
but no one comes knocking,
like the fear of acknowledging
is even worse than then the simple act of asking
if I'm okay. What happened to the world
where people care?

Momma,
it hurts how much I care.
Do you see the cuts there?
Why won't you ask?
Why won't you care? Momma,
this heart is too open and these hands are too freely healing others.
This mouth won't stop talking, and Momma,
I feel the emotions crashing into me.
I just want love Momma, and you won't give it to me
so I have to find it in someone else.

But Momma,
the boys are mean to me.
They slam my skull into the wall
and watch as pain decorates

my eyes, laughing
because control is the one thing in their lives
that they can gain from me.
Momma, the boys are cruel, they sit beside me in school
and pretend they know me,
they pretend I have more to me than just a body.
Momma what do I do for a boy who just wants my body?
I try to care.
I try to teach them that there's more to it than this.
But they don't see beneath.

Momma, this boy hates himself.
What do I do for a boy that hates himself?

Momma, I'm sick.
I'm so sick of this fever called wanting love
that I just want to carve it out
of my heart sometimes
and lay the emotions to rest
in a coffin beside my traumatic memories.
He needs me to stay.
Momma, text me back.
His arms are around my neck.
Momma,
I don't want to ignore, he needs me,
Momma are you listening to me?

Momma,
I need you to help me.
Momma, I
need you to love me.

Mom,
"Are you listening?"
"Sorry what was that?"
"Never mind."

#31

Words now
alight my
conscious, and I was
slipping—
                    slipping
between
                    reality

and dysfunction,
                    slipping

between

                    the universe's fingers,

you needed to curtain close
        the light as it interrogated
        the dark.
I needed
        to close
my heart for business
        if it kept me alive.

I need
        to board up
        these ears
        so I cannot hear the words
I once kept saying.

You know the ones
where I gave you the light
        so you could curtain
close the dark from
playing bad cop
to the sun?

I cut off these
ears from sound—
         the ones
where my whimper
         is soft and dainty
pressed to my lips
like wallflowers hanging in the background
not wanting to overstep
         their bounds.

Though, be warned,
these lips
learned to speak
         powerfully and with purpose.
         This flower learned to climb walls,
I can now admit that.

Part IV

(Deserted) #32

All of the
sirens must have been
asleep that night.

The graffiti man's face
must have come alive,
and crept to the other
side of the wall—because anyone looking
        would have known
        this wasn't right.

I stayed—
        because I
        care too deep—
more than the
ocean
sometimes.
I love potential—
to which always   kills
                        me.

I stayed

                because homeless souls,
                & wounded hearts, I can
                lull to see
                worth and beauty
                in themselves—
and to that
I will *never*
give up.

But I stayed—
with you   that night
to keep you
from

            You.
But You
could not reach you, so You
came after me; all of Me.

All of the
world must have
turned off
their lights—
because there was not
a shred
of one showing me
the way out
of   your dark rooms.

Not one sliver
of sky stealing
        me away
        from your eyes.

Why?
Why are those
never around
when you need them the most?

Why did it take
until 6 am for someone
to   respond
                to my plea?

Sometimes,
I feel I am still
screaming—out into
the blue—
but no one

ever comes

after me.

I stayed—
        because that's what
        I do.

But I'd rather have done
that, then disobeyed
my nature,
and left you
           to die
           alone.
I stayed—
and You stayed
inside.

The world
must have forgotten
what it means
to be Good.

The world
must have forgotten
to send a life raft…

Some days—
I'm still waiting
for it to
appear.

#33

You cut
me open with your hands. You sliced
myself from me. Is it worth it, to be alive?
Lungs are out of tune instruments, breathe
me air, *please*. Love
me, to help save me. Die

to be reborn. I died
when your lips moved to make words for me. I've never been in
love.
My body a sweater you cut—
to shreds, exposure I didn't think I minded… until you sliced—
a hole in my back. Metaphorically (too). Into your lungs I breathe
smoke, yes, you killed—brought me alive.

A living
person breathes. Definition seems lacking to me, dying
to know the real, truth. Cut
open like a nut. Hard to crack, to love—but, was willing to slice
you undone anyway. I must learn to breathe—

I thought you might teach me. Love
me back to life. Force my bones to move, to be alive
again. Slice
up my fears, die
with me. But you're afraid how deep I'll cut
you with my saw of a heart. Breathing—

smoke back into my lungs. Breathe,
remember to, often times I forget. Loving
the feeling of being cut
open again. Live
to die.
Slice

off the flaws you don't like. A slice
of me, a sweet treat, you thought you could purchase. Breathe
my phantom air, you are no longer here. Die
memories, fade into spirits with no control onto how I love.
Scream into my third eye if you must, alive
means I am living *without you*. These cuts

from you have healed. Cutting stone, a grave for you. It's easier to
breathe.
I'm harder to please, thicker with each slice. No longer seeking
love.
For myself, I have discovered it. Alive to *live*, no longer to die.

#34

I
am still
able to breathe
regardless
of your hands
choking
me.

I am
still
able to
work
these lungs,
regardless
of the words
you shoved inside them
regardless
of the abuse
you may have used
as weapons.

I am still able
to speak,
miraculously
you know,
throat chakra
has a hard time
healing after
what has been
done.

I am still
able to
say
your name,

regardless
of how much I
want to erase
it from
my vocabulary.

I am
still
able.

I am
still.

I am.

I am.

Thank god,
I am.

#35

Next year has to be better,
this   awful year
is ending.
          And then
I can stop pretending
that I am
          still living it.

Maybe my eyes
in 2018
will learn just how
to move
without looking behind
my spine.

Wouldn't it be wonderful,
if this body could sway
without hips
warning themselves
what the men
around night
do with their hands,
if I walk close enough to
the darkness of alleyways?

Wouldn't it be great
          if my face
didn't need to be covered
by strands of hair
          without feeling vulnerable—completely bare,
afraid
you might
see me again?

Maybe in 2018

these limbs
won't   grow
out of chains, maybe these bones
won't rattle against the prison
of my chest,
          maybe these insides
won't feel as if they
were born
inside of a horror flick.
Maybe next year
          I can smile, without flinching
immediately after because
to be happy is a temporary distraction.

Wouldn't it be nice?
If my veins
weren't so hell bent on
          pulsating right below
the places
your thumb pushed
me
against my will?

Wouldn't it be fabulous,
          if this skin
you touched on my neck
didn't want to creep off of
my body and separate
into some other being,
because sometimes
I feel I don't belong
in my own skin?

Maybe in 2018
I will remember what it feels like
be inside myself
once again.

Maybe I will remember
what it feels like
to be
me
again.

#36

I grow my strength
on my biceps,
I run from you
        on treadmills: preparing
for battle.
I should be in the best shape,
so if I ever face you again,
        I won't sit there like a little girl
afraid of what her fists can do,
mistaking what her feet have to say
        about staying.

When I see you again,
if I ever do,
        you better have been training too,
because it will not be a fair
fight if you haven't.

#37

Do my eyelids keep
twitching because
I have forced myself
to stay awake
during the night
so that I don't dream of my
fear for you
      you—
      you—
you—inside
      my head.

You are inside
my eyes,
no longer
do I find paradise in retreating
in them, instead,
      I journey only
back down
to hell.

#38

If you look in my eyes
would you see
the deceit I believed?

Or did you just
project such
self-loathing onto me?
Perhaps this is why
you hit me?
You mistook my face
with your own,
but were too much
of a coward to brave
your own pain—
so instead
you caused all of
mine.

#39

Were you lost when
you came to earth or did
you choose this life
you created?

Surely you must
have realized your mistake
when they tried to
ship you back
to where you came from?

#40

If there were ever
a moment that this mind
was one
you cared for at all
tell me—

I thought we were best friends,
you said we were.
Tell me—

Did you ever rethink
the plot you strategized
when you decided
to ruin all of me?

#41

Was the darkness enough?
Or did you have to slink inside
the holes of my sky
just to fool your integrity
that you were alive?

#42

I bet when you stepped
on those   roses outside
and dumped your ash tray
into their roots   they tried
hexing you.

I bet when they did
        you felt the betrayal of the world
like just another day.

#43

Your arms were hungry
as they
devoured my skin
like a dish
I   never
intended
on serving.

#44

Ever since you
       this rose
has just kept on
sprouting thorns.

#45

The moon makes
me out to be a saint.
But does the sun understand
the pain associated with
the memories
dripping like acid
from between these legs?

#46

The stars may have thought
I surrendered
but there is
a radiance inside
me
that will outmatch
his.

They laugh suddenly,
"How funny you think
we ever believed
you didn't?"

#47

I remember the birthdays
of celebrating myself,
but you have made me
not want to.

Now I often confuse
        joyful balloons with
        painful memories
of clinging onto
        some string of sanity.

#48

I often forget
      a time
ever filled with
      vain
and not a bundle
of dark vivid metaphors.

#49

The tears
tear at my cheeks
opening up a portal
stretching it
open for me
to burrow myself
inside of,

is that what it felt
like when
you went   inside too?

#50

Do you know
who I am
now?

Or was I just
part of your collection
of women
who you screwed?

And are we now
put under a glass
case of your memories,
so you could remember
us women
when you ejaculate?

#51

He covered my
lips,
but this
voice
didn't stop talking
even as he did.

He cut off
any oxygen
that could be
pulled in.
Even as my brain lost
knowledge of where
I was, who I was,
I never stopped
fighting.

#52

Maybe you knew
        who I really was inside.
Maybe you were sent down
        to steal my light for yourself?
You held my wings
and ripped them off my
back, leaving bloody
disfigured stems.

Now I don't know
how to escape
or what it even means
to fly.

I remember
what my true nature once was,
and I guess
I'm searching for
ways to grow back
a part of myself,
and heal   the truth that
remains.

#53

Just because I am "better"
does not mean
        I have forgotten.

        Just because I don't
talk about it
doesn't mean I don't
still feel it.

Just because I am healing,
        doesn't mean the wound
doesn't still bleed sometimes.

#54

You leave me
        paralyzed even
a year later, body squished
up like a child
holding my insides
in so they don't spill out
onto the floor. Would I ever reclaim them
if they did?

I push the spots on my neck
that used to contain the dark
        cloud of bruises, they sometimes
black out my vision from time to time,
the phantom pain resurfacing.
        Even as it will be one
year a week from my birthday,
        I'm waiting for
the flashbacks
        to arise like gifts.

I found the shirt I wore
        last year, and tossed it in the trash,
"current mood" scrawled on the front. Was
I conveying something that night?
        Was it the way the shirt cut a little
too low? You had to know
        it wasn't my intention when it fell off my shoulders,
you had to know it wasn't a display of any sort
of affection. You had to know pink wasn't
        a color that intended for
your hands to take
        what was mine, and never
never
        yours.

A year later
        I can't move
this skeleton from
where it sits in
the traps of mind,
        my brain seems
to want to play the movie
over and over,
and I have been chained to
the theater seats against my will—
        I can't keep watching as
you thrust into me,
        "You wanted this. You asked for this."

No
no
no I didn't.

Yes you did.

And it's like I'm having
conversations with your spirit
so close to my ear,
        but you are not here,
        you are not here,
you are not here,
you are not here.

Yes I am, you wanted this. You asked for this.

I didn't. Please, I
never wanted
this.

#55

I've healed.
I've grown,
but that's not to say I forget.
The cries at night   still shout.
The times my mind   screamed stop   still yell,
but my mouth couldn't
function to form the words,   so I hear it now.

I'm healing.
I'm frowning.
I'm kind. I'm me again.
I took back my strength.
but I still can't trust, and
somewhere there is
this dark gaping hole still
inside.

I've grown.
I'm developing.
I'm healing my heart
mind and soul. I'm confident
this skin is
only for those who respect it,
doesn't mean I'm
not terrified
of sex   still.

There are some things
that only time
is able to grow,
heal, and allow me
to move forward from.

Until then,
I'll keep

healing, keep growing
and keep learning
how to forgive myself.

#56

The moon
was full that night.

I remember seeing it,
        hating it
for being so full, while
        all of me was being
sucked out,
        taken.

The moon was full,
        the glow was impeccable,
and I felt the halo of
        innocence being
darkened by his
        shades.

The moon was full,
        and illuminating
after he had
gone to sleep leaving me in
fear that if I had left;
        he would have killed himself—

The moon was full
        of apologies, telling me
to stay tethered to it,
        extending a light
in all of
        the darkness.

#57

The moon
          & stars
wept while
the tears
          engraved craters
under these eyes.

Moon extended his glow
          so my body would have
something to hold onto
besides the sight
of   him
inside.

The stars
          wrapped each other
in hugs, coming together
during this scene,
          dust falling from
their magic, and coating the windows
with fog.

The moon & stars
witnessed my rape,
          and when the night became
too dark, moon handed
          me off to the sun, praying
that she could
          give me back my light
from which I had lost.

#58

My mind
holds me
bare,
you think
it would protect
me against
myself.

You think
I would know better,
that my mind
would pursue other
routes in which
to journey down.

You would think when
you are taken
prisoner, at least
you would know when
the act was being done.
I did not.

"Are you a screamer?" I wonder
if he asked this question.
I wonder if the scar on my back
was a gentle incision
as if he were a scientist
injecting me with
his latest experiment.

I wondered
If I came
when he hit me that
hard with his maleness,
and I loathe myself

to think that I might have.

I wonder
what conversations
we had, when he gave me more to drink.
He said that I begged for it.
He told me we had sex
three times, *that night*
did we have more? Did you lie?

I don't remember much,
I guess I'm lucky, or so they think.
I can only recall a few moments,
But sometimes my mind
gives me back moments
when it thinks I'm ready
to handle them:
like little pieces of time,
him inside,
        power over me, no control.

"Are you afraid?"
I wonder if my brain
asked me that.
"Are you alright?"
I wondered if I asked
myself that.

You stole
this skin from me.
You stole
my trust from me.
You kidnapped,
and tortured my heart, my body.
You took that night
from me.

Do you know we
only have so many days
and nights to live?
I bet you don't
even recall the act,
or the night of taking
everything
from me.

I bet you think
you got away with it.
They all think
they got away
with it.

"You survived."
Yes, I did. Doesn't mean
the wounds don't still lurk,
don't still hurt. Do you know scars
can still affect the body when we know
they shouldn't?
When we know the past
has passed, but it's still
here following? Stalking? Haunting?

"You're alive."
Yes, but sometimes
it feels like I am not living,
because of you.
I may breathe air,
and speak,
but some days
it feels like that
is all
I am doing.

"Are you doing better?"

Yes.
But will I forget?   Never.
How does one forget
when someone violates their body?
When the choices
they have been given
are extracted from them without their knowledge?
When their voices
are stripped of sound, and
drained to last breath?
When their essence, their trust
is mutated, butchered,
when horrible things occur,
how do you forget?

You don't.
But that doesn't mean
that they win.
No,
that means
that I have taken
the steps, *no*,
I have worked through the
pain, and yes there is always
going to be more.
There will always
be a remembrance of him,
but he does not get
to win.

What is won
is the building back.
The broken building
being reconstructed
by self, and respect.
The construction of heart
being melded together

by the essence of
our strength.
The sculpting of
our own bodies
with our own hands,
we do not feel
theirs building us
for their own.
We were not made
for their pleasure
alone.

We were born
for the beauty
of ourselves, of our choices
to who we are
and how we live, and
how we are treated.
They do not win,
because they will
never harm
us
again.

We
will *always*
make sure of it.

#59

I folded my kindness
up into little notes
addressed to hearts
that have lacked in it.

I packaged up my love
stuffing tissue paper
of compassion, tightly taping
my voice shut.
This way you could
open me up and
see what was inside.

But I discovered
all the letters stamped with positivity
and purity
were piled up on
the doorstep of my soul.

And maybe
it was a profound mistake
of mine to include the return address.

Because now
I open the envelope containing my old selves
and with nurturing arms
I store them back
in the shelves
of this body.

And maybe, throughout all this
I was the present
being given back
to myself.

ABOUT THE AUTHOR

I live in Maryland, work as a Reiki Practitioner and am currently working on my Bachelor's Degree in Creative Writing. I also work for Passager Books as the Editorial Assistant. My work has been published in two literary journals: *The Muse* at Howard Community College, and *Skelter* at University of Baltimore. I have also been published in *Maryland's Best Emerging Poets: An Anthology.* I am twenty-two years old and have been writing all of my life. I declared it my major when I realized I could not live without it.

Made in the USA
Middletown, DE
23 May 2019